Excellent Reading Report Comments for Your Child

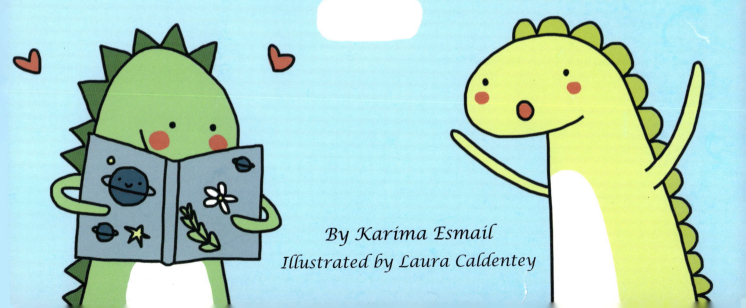

By Karima Esmail
Illustrated by Laura Caldentey

JellyJames Publishing Ltd
19 Cumberland Road, Stanmore
Middlesex HA7 1EL, England

©JellyJames Publishing Ltd 2014

ISBN 978-1-90413-416-9

All rights reserved. No part of this publication may be reproduced, stored in a retrieval system, or transmitted in any form or by any means, electronic, mechanical, photocopying or otherwise, without the prior written permission of JellyJames Publishing Ltd.
A catalogue record of this book is available from the British Library.

www.readingrecord.co.uk

About the author

Karima Esmail is an experienced and respected author of educational books and interactive software. She previously taught as a Senior Lecturer at the University of Hertfordshire and has published literacy and numeracy resources that address the needs of diverse learners. These have been translated into many languages and are being used internationally.

She has two children who are successful and happy professionals. Whilst they were at school, she loved writing comments detailing her children's reading progress in their diaries and received overwhelmingly positive feedback from teachers. She has now decided to share these comments with parents so that they too experience this enjoyment.

About the illustrator

When Laura Caldentey was little she couldn't live without her crayon box, now she can't live without her drawing tablet.
After studying Media she always knew that she wanted to draw, so she started working as a freelancer and building her online shop, and as that little girl never imagined, she ended up having commissioned work from international clients across the globe.

Laura works from her cosy studio in Palma de Mallorca, very near to the beautiful Mediterranean sea. The nature and people from her beloved island are the main inspiration for her work.

Omar was so excited to read his very first book from school.

Jemma and her dad enjoyed reading the book together.

We loved discussing the story and talking about what was happening.

Nahema read the words loudly and clearly.
She wanted to repeat them over and over again!

Lee attempted to read the tricky words by sounding out the letters.

Kishan used the clues in the pictures to identify unknown words.

Oliver can identify individual sounds in words.

Amy can read words by blending sounds together.

John recognised the words on the flashcards.

I am so impressed with Aziza's motivation to sound out words.

Paul knew that sentences are read from left to right.

It was such a pleasure to listen to Jane read.
She was able to identify the words independently.

Helen spotted a full stop!

Bella drew a lovely picture of the house.

Read the book enthusiastically, clearly and with understanding.

Fluent and confident, showing enthusiasm and enjoyment.

Confused 'b' and 'd' sounds at the beginning of the word 'dig' but self-corrected when read within the context of the sentence. Wonderful!

Shazia recognised the exclamation mark!

The tools on page 8 helped us explore the story further.

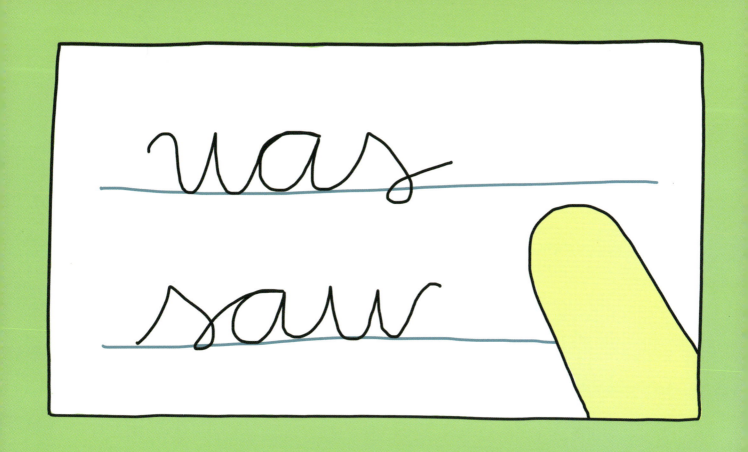

Tends to mistake 'was' with 'saw'.

Khaliya loved the pictures and we enjoyed discussing them together.

Harry is now recognising words far more easily.

Ziyana found the word 'after' very tricky.

As he read, he recognised and followed the punctuation.

Wow! First story read to the end with no help whatsoever.

Found this book quite easy.

Could you please review the level of her book as she found it quite challenging.

This series is proving to be the most challenging so far. Mary is learning new words every day and is thoroughly enjoying the adventure theme.

She is beginning to discuss the book.

Read effortlessly!

We looked at the title and Sharon felt that it did not fit the book!

James was totally absorbed in his reading.

We recorded Tom's reading and played it back.
He loved listening to himself read.

Read at a steady pace and with enjoyment.

Grandma was over the moon when she heard Emily read!

I am delighted that his reading confidence has increased leaps and bounds!

Gina noticed that the front cover had pictures in colour, unlike the inside of the book.

Predicting what will happen next proved challenging and we started the thinking process for Terry.

Mela is making wonderful progress with her reading and amazes me with how she is tackling harder words.

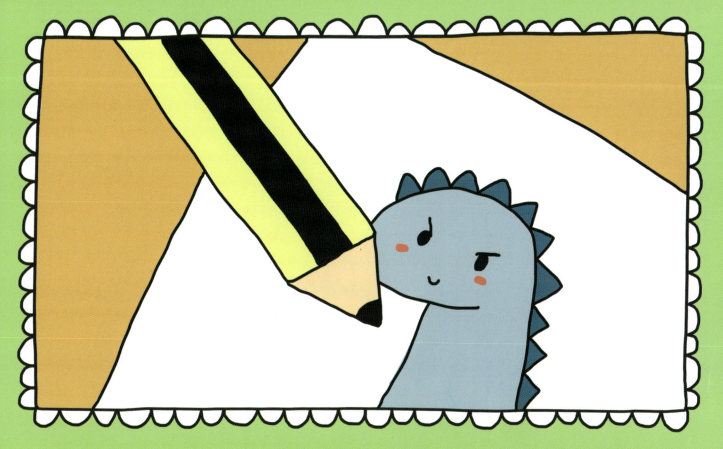

Whilst drawing the picture, she was keen to show the naughty side of the character!

Noor was pleased that the ending was happy!

Rosa enjoyed the story and was keen to share her own experience.

Diana was upset when Grace could not find her mum, but was relieved when they were reunited at the end.

Laura attempted the Learning tool on page 25 using sounds and words that she was familiar with.

Read beautifully with lots of expression. Brilliant!

Needed a little encouragement this evening to remain focused.

Wonderful! Made extremely good attempt at 'sounding out' unfamiliar words.

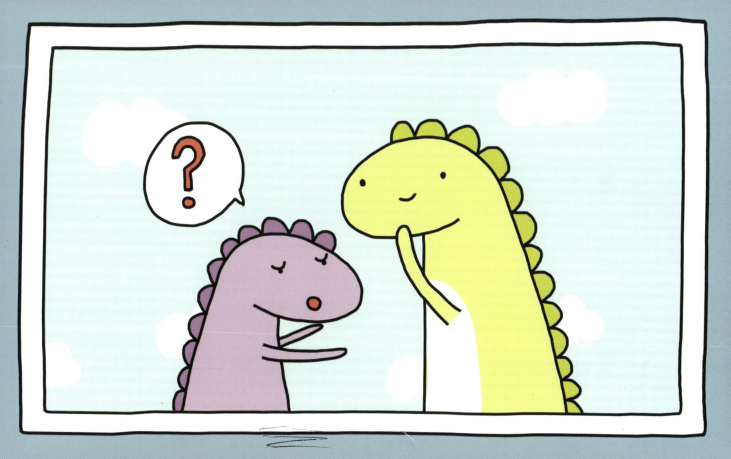

Asked many relevant questions about the story and characters - great!

Aliya really enjoyed this book set by the sea. It reminded her of the Lighthouse Keeper books.

Rahim particularly enjoyed reading this book and looking at the illustrations.

Very little help needed today. Remembered many of the letter sounds and read lots of words independently.

Lovely reading and only a little help needed today!

Noor, you read the book at a lovely pace and effortlessly. You are now a better reader than me!

Really impressed! You should feel very proud. It was an absolute pleasure listening to you read.

Neal, I am thrilled with your reading.
You are a super reader!

Notes

Notes